The Moment's Gold

by the same author:

AN EVER FIXÉD MARK (1973)

The Moment's Gold

*"I'll glean the moment's
gold for you to share . . ."*

Mary Spain

SHEPHEARD-WALWYN

First published 1974

ISBN 0 85683 012 7

Printed and bound in Great Britain by
Staples Printers Ltd., Rochester, Kent
for Shepheard-Walwyn (Publishers) Ltd.,
56 Doughty Street, London WC1N 2LS

Foreword

As a writer and painter, I find '*The Moment's Gold*' pure enchantment. I, too, am intrigued by nature and its passing seasons, and delight in sharing Mary Spain's Winter-to-Winter impressions. There is a frugal beauty in her work.

I

Introduction

It almost seems as though I cannot write
Except for you. What little talent I
Possess is not my own, but knows delight
In rising from some hidden source to cry
Obedience to your command. You need
To smile ? Then let it cast its net and catch
You gaiety. You yearn for love to feed
Your hungry heart ? Then shall its bow despatch
A quiverful of joy to minister
And care. A talent knows no selfish aim
And only shines when polished by the spur
Of need; a teasing gem that none can claim
To own. In recognition of this law
My willing pen will serve you evermore.

II

A city street, one hour before the dawn,
Cheerless with winter's chill. I hurry past
Anonymous closed doors; a cat, forlorn
And wary, turns its head; within the vast
And silent concrete labyrinth my feet
Beat rhythmic echo, echo on the ground.
Then, all at once, the dark and dream-locked street
Is wakened from inertia by a sound.
As though it were the countryside at dawn
A single bird gives greeting to the day;
Up, up into the night his song is borne
On light of grace that darkness cannot stay.
Can man's ideas of space and time be true
If that small bird I heard now sings for you?

III

With pen and paper may I share with you
This Winter scene? Imagine, as I write,
A river bank, a sky of gentle blue,
A robin's song, a drift of snowdrops, white
And tremb'ling 'neath the trees. A scene as clear,
As fine as though it were eternally
Engraved on glass. One would not speak for fear
A sound might break the moment's harmony.
Words cannot place the moss beneath your feet,
Nor fill your lungs with Oxfordshire's sweet air,
Nor sound the chuckle where the waters meet,
Nor thread the silver sunlight through your hair,
But you, my love, can recreate in mind
More beauty than these words could ever find.

IV

A vision growing, swelling, held within
Resistant case; a promise whispering
Its message, louder, louder 'til the thin,
Pale cheeks of Winter glow with thoughts of Spring.
Rhythmic tension mounting, mounting; movement
Captive, seeking freedom; life in darkness
'Til the joyous, long-awaited moment
Of release. So the buds, through sun's caress
Which penetrates dark Winter's shield, burst free
In fragile finery. I can't ignore
This upsurge in my heart, this buoyancy
Of mind and step that wasn't there before.
Is it just Spring I have to thank for this,
Or life itself which offers happiness ?

V

Let not my love be limited to my
Poor pen; I will entrust its bounty to
The elements that light and air shall vie
For place to be my messengers. To you
I'll come on every eastern breeze; when sun
Lights on your face it is my kiss that knows
The need for warmth within your heart; and shun
Not rain, for out of every drop there flows
Such gentle benison that you will see
No space divides us but is thickly knit
With pulsing arteries of love. Give me
Your word that when, beside the fire, you sit
Alone you will recall I lit the flame;
Then, softly, in the silence, speak my name.

VI

My temporal span of youth had passed away
When you bestowed on me a second Spring.
Not bound by time and destined for decay,
But love's eternal, ageless offering.
Though I'll grow old, my dear, for mortals age
And passing years leave trace ere they depart,
Yet will I spurn time's tyranny to stage
A scene of endless Springtime in your heart.
I'd not return to that first youth, when shy
And on my guard I stumbled from the nest;
But such the joys of second Spring that I
Have shed defences and to love confessed.
You brought me youth, I can but offer this,
That in my arms you'll share love's timeless bliss.

VII

Sweet-scented innocents with golden eyes,
Deep-throated choristers who sing in praise;
Tell me, narcissi, why life's turmoil dies
When in simplicity I rest my gaze
Upon your purity ? With trust you face
The world, and give my room no less of your
Clear beauty than it were your tranquil place
Of birth. With such abundance do you pour
Your wealth that even in the darkness I
Feel sure your flame of life must radiate
Its light, as joy illuminates the eye
Of those who may your grace participate.
I rest on you, and see my inner bliss
Reflected in five-petalled happiness.

VIII

The world I see is me; all creatures show
Fresh facets of myself. I recognise
A smile or frown because my nature knows
Their worth. If beauty rests within men's eyes
Reflect, my darling, qualities ascribed
By you to me must firstly dwell in you;
My little virtue yours has magnified,
Through your clear gaze my inner light shines through.
Your love looked down upon the commonplace
And saw its own sweet nature hidden there;
And I, reflecting mirror to love's grace,
Acquired a radiance that all may share.
An ordinary woman, but for this,
That I have been exalted by your kiss.

IX

Some florists take fresh rose-buds and, with wire,
Prevent their promised blooms from opening.
Yet youth cannot be chained, it will expire
Imprisoned in an artificial Spring.
Age need not mean decline, for life will grow
To rich maturity 'neath Autumn skies.
And how can new-born Springtime ever know
The deep fulfilment that the fruit supplies ?
Each season has its special role to play,
A part well-ordered by creation's law;
Within the seed was planned the leaf's decay
As surely as the first frail shoot it bore.
I will not weep when Summer's blooms are shed
If Autumn's glory beckons me ahead.

X

There was a time when each of us knew birth,
A time is set for each of us to die,
And, inbetween, we sojourners to earth
Must to the seasons of this earth comply.
No use in hankering for Autumn gold
When Springtime buds are bursting on the bough;
No sense anticipating joys foretold
Ignoring that the fount of joy is now.
To wish away today is to deny
The unrepeated knowledge this day yields;
Yet how impatiently I often sigh
For greener grass that grows in future fields.
I will not ask what destiny has planned,
Some day, in God's good time, I'll understand.

XI

Together on the train, but separate;
Eight bodies brought into proximity
That nudge and jostle with the shifting weight.
The city worker seated next to me
Considers racing prospects for the day;
I write to you; a grey-haired lady reads
Her book; the others take the chance to sway
In sleep. Here for an hour. Have we no needs
That each might satisfy ? No common link
But shared humanity ? Must each one glance
Away if eyes should meet lest any think
He sought to make a tentative advance ?
Our destination reached we rise to go,
And what each might have shared we'll never know.

XII

You said you'd think of me; but was there need
To tell me so ? Have you not realised
Your thoughts inform my heart with greater speed
Than any words ? Thoughts travel not disguised
As speech may do. With sunlit clarity
Yours reconfirm our love, and seem so near
That in response mine chatter happily,
Rejoicing in the knowledge that you're here.
I glean the moment's gold for you to share,
And inextricably you are a part
Of all the good, and memorable, and rare
That serve to gladden and sustain my heart.
You said you'd think of me. Each time you do
Remember that my thoughts will be of you.

XIII

Long shadows on the grass proclaim the dawn,
The Winter is but herald to the Spring;
From out of death is hope of life reborn,
From out of sleep must come awakening.
Without the darkness who could speak of light ?
Can man know hope who has not known despair;
Or, without any option, choose the right;
Or, without isolation, learn to share ?
If black and white as matching halves are seen,
And pain and pleasure cannot live apart,
Duality's apparent coloured screen
Dissolves to show creation's single heart.
A single dreaming heart that peoples space
With all the fantasies of time and place.

XIV

On Summer afternoons, from two to four,
The sunshine's probing fingers gently trace
A passage 'twixt the city roofs to pour
In fullness on a basement dwelling place.
Here, tended by the occupant within,
A little garden manages to grow.
Each corner for a pot or earth-filled tin
Is utilised; and from these efforts flow
Such unexpected Summer flowers that we
Who pass, heads bent and lost in thought, for this
Brief moment waken from our dreams to see
A world made brighter by such loveliness.
A little garden ? No! My heart denies
That such a paradise be judged by size.

XV

Yes; it will be the perfume I remember,
When time has caused the visual feast to fade;
Translucent pink to carmine and magenta,
The softest green to emerald and jade.
When mem'ry has forgotten the profusion
As regiments of blooms stood ranked in rows,
Assembled here the flowers of every nation,
The edelweiss, the lily and the rose.
When they have closed the age-old city market
Proclaiming needs of progress, it will be
As scented air at daybreak I'll recall it,
Inviting us to rouse from reverie.
When demolition ceases shall we find
A gentle waft of perfume left behind ?

XVI

A sea of living crimson caught my eye
Of oriental splendour, out of place
Beneath the pastel of an English sky
Where soft-toned pastures etch the tranquil face
Of Summertime. A silken, poppied sea
That shimmered in the early morning sun,
And with true beauty's generosity
Held out its cup of joy to everyone.
The sober hedgerows glowed a richer hue,
The willow-herb a dainty blush revealed,
And I have never seen a sky as blue
As that which smiled upon the poppy field.
Sweet flowers that bring men sleep, you brought to me
A wakened joy that lives in memory.

XVII

Forgetful of the light, we move below
As thoughts beneath the surface of the mind,
Cocooned in darkness; satisfied to know
The names of passing stations as the blind
Know landmarks. Yet, not far away, birds wheel
In open skies, the noisy traffic sings
Its strident chorus overhead. We steal
In silent convoys, unaware of things
Above, until, our destination gained,
We blink acceptance of the brighter light
Forgetting those companions who've remained,
Still travelling beneath us, out of sight.
Two worlds that seek their privacy to keep?
Or one that we inhabit half-asleep?

XVIII

We move as clouds that merge, and separate,
And merge again; of substance uniform,
Our ways identical. We cannot wait
Or alter course at will. Within the storm
We seek the silent heart that will remain
When thunder's rage has passed. Not our's to change
Creation's face, nor have we to explain
Its mysteries; we simply watch the range
And scope of its complexity and know
That, like ourselves, as moving clouds that merge,
And separate, and merge again, the flow
Of life is one. Let us upon the surge
Of love draw near that we may recognise
The one true light that shines from out our eyes.

XIX

Across a gap, that is not there, I reach
To speak to you, though you are one with me;
Loose sentences I throw across the breach
To span the chasm of duality.
Trust guides my feet along this frail support,
Truth holds my head erect that I may see
Not isolation that ideas have wrought
But, in your steadfast gaze, love's unity.
And yet this bridge will bear no surplus weight:
All must be laid aside if I'm to cross.
One ounce of selfishness will separate
Our outstretched hands; a claim results in loss.
A life-time's luggage must we jettison
To learn the simple truth that two are one.

XX

Speech sails uncertain on an unknown sea,
Wind-borne and hesitant, intent to gain
The harbour of a list'ning ear. Though free
How often will we bind a golden chain
About each word, reluctant to let go
Lest by communication we should be
Diminished. Thus the willing, outward flow
Is checked, and laden with despondency
Each crippled craft returns from whence it came.
Yet may the eyes the inner soul relate,
Once we have cleansed them of desire to claim,
As, piercing time and space, they radiate
Our unity. Dear love, I'll not forget
Those wordless, bliss-filled moments when we've met.

XXI

I heard a wise man say: "When I have gone
Mourn not what might have been. Remember you
Are caring for me still by going on
In search of truth, as I would wish you to."
How great the span of love; it is not bound
By simple service to the body's needs
But hungers for the knowledge to be found
In richer pastures where the spirit feeds.
I love you as I seek to follow right;
I love you when I overcome distress,
When I accept with grace those facts that might
So easily give rise to bitterness.
Through loving you, my dear, I'll hope to be
In some part worthy of your love for me.

XXII

Slow, Summer days that slip away into
The drowsy twilight's welcoming embrace.
Soft, sun-bleached skies whose parasol of blue
Reflects the tranquil bloom on Summer's face.
Still, still the air that cradles on its wing
The orchestrated chant of sun-drunk bees;
And butterflies, so gaily fluttering,
Like polka dots held captive by the breeze.
Time holds its breath on reaching Summer's peak;
I hear the grasses whispering that this
Full moment holds the clue to all I seek,
A wordless, timeless, golden happiness.
Contained in earth, by sun and water blessed,
The Summer and my spirit come to rest.

XXIII

A Summer twilight, one small cat alone
Amongst the tombstones, gaily wandering,
Intent on mice and moths, and hardly prone
To flights of fancy; just meandering
Alone . . . when she stopped. I will never know
What held her there. Or why she stood, fur raised,
Listening, whilst her wide eyes seemed to grow
Half mesmerised; not fearful but amazed.
The leaning tombstone told of Emily
Who'd died in youth on this day long ago.
No mention made of friends or family;
Had she a cat ? Before I turned to go
I laid some woodland flowers in memory
Of this forgotten anniversary.

XXIV

Arise to life, cold stone; soft blossoms drift
Across your waxen cheek and make it glow.
Sweet fragrance stirs the air and wild flowers lift
Frail heads in songs of praise as though they know
Of immortality. Here lies a knight
Who's waited centuries for roses o'er
His heart; his lady smiles in sleep as might
One smile who sleeps on petal-pillowed floor.
Rejoice, cold stone; man's craftmanship and skill
Responds to nature's art and, in reply,
Enhances natural loveliness as will
A compliment shy beauty magnify.
Thus Summer's fleeting glory can impart
To ancient, lifeless masonry a heart.

XXV

Forgotten jungles fired those blazing eyes,
Whilst from the throat an ancient memory
Gives utterance to low, staccato cries.
Attention that before roamed wide and free
Now centres on a point. All consciousness
Is focused, clear and still; no time but now,
No aim in mind but this. With suppleness
Of liquid steel the crouching limbs allow
Their tension to escape through twitching tail.
No worries drain the body's energy;
No idle thoughts of failure can prevail
To blur that cloudless mental clarity.
At last, with lethal, calculated spring,
The kitten pounces on the ball of string.

XXVI

When love was young I held you to my breast
And thought with body's gift I offered all;
How joyfully my lips on yours found rest,
How eagerly my feet obeyed your call.
But mind denied desire for mastery
And, like rebellious infant, sought its way
By female guile and soft cajolery
Pretending that it wanted to obey.
If I have seen the truth that flesh is one
Why must I fight for mind's identity?
What is this battle that I think I've won
When wilfulness has severed unity?
Should deathless Eve attempt to gain control
Remind me, darling, of her proper role.

XXVII

I shone the light of reason on our love,
Half fearful that such brilliance might show
A flaw within its beauty, and thus prove
My heart to be unwise to love you so.
But reason only fed the mental fire
That blazes from two minds that act as one,
And unity appeared not from desire
But from true knowledge of our union.
Whilst in my heart I hid my love away
Yet reason called it forth to light my face,
And none who sees this happiness could say
Such love is other than a gift of grace.
So doubt me not, my darling; who are we
To question what our hearts and minds agree?

XXVIII

Say not that beauty's dead, for you are wrong;
Behold the countless facets of her face.
See morning workers interweave along
The streets in measured dance of speed and grace;
Dust particles in sunlit liberty;
Rain in the lamp-light; silent cranes at dawn;
Vast cooling towers in slumb'rous majesty
Against the sky; steel bridges, finely-drawn,
Which in their liquid arcs make music. Hear
At break of day the city's waking note;
The song as metals meet; whilst rhythm clear
Stems forth from powerful engine's vibrant throat.
Abundant beauty casts her net so wide
That all is held, and nought remains outside.

XXIX

A seed lies in my hand, shrivelled and lined,
Such humble home for cosmic mystery;
Yet, deep within this scrap of dust we find
The essence of a world. Of limits free
It can extend its scope to cedar's span,
Or etch the subtle beauties of a rose.
But, analyse this seed, it yields no plan.
Where wait the colours that the artist knows?
Where lurks the scent that rides the Summer breeze?
Are they but whispers waiting on a breath
Whose potent magic activates and frees
This wrinkled granule from the dreams of death?
Know you, small seed, the seed that knows us all;
Still point of our creation and recall?

XXX

The scientists in solemn conclave met,
Each bearing theses on the laws of flight.
That man had reached the moon they knew, but yet
Was there some flaw, some vital oversight?
The subject of their joint anxiety,
Who posed a query non-one could deny:
None other than the humble bumble-bee
Who, by all laws they knew, should never fly.
Those fragile wings could barely lift a flea;
That they should raise such bulk was quite absurd.
Yet how to reason with a trusting bee
Who, thinking it can fly, soars like a bird?
If faith can give the bee such liberty
What might I not achieve through trust in Thee?

XXXI

"We'll take you up to see the view," they said.
And so we journeyed through the Autumn rain,
The children wishing they had played instead;
Their weary parents trying to explain,
With fraying patience, how they ought to show
Their aunt the countryside. Five people, set
Apart by irritation, huddled low
Within the car. We got out on the wet,
Sweet grass a very fractious cavalcade;
'Til, over-awed by space, dissension died,
And clouded eyes awoke to see displayed
The patient glory of the countryside.
As mortals changed, we stood in silence there;
And five were one, and one was everywhere.

XXXII

Quiet, self-effacing craft; the needle's art
Knows care and discipline, not vanity.
It pleads no cause, unburdens not its heart,
Portraying truth with simple clarity.
What joy to rest the eye on pure design,
What artless gaiety in crimson thread,
How delicate the gold and silver line,
The sequins nestling in their silken bed.
Here slip-stitch, chain-stitch, satin-stitch entwine
And merge as single drops in common sea.
Here craft and colour, care and form combine
To show how many strands make unity.
Amongst the graces of our human race
Who can deny the gentle needle's place?

XXXIII

Housed in the framework of poetic law
There dwells a thought. So small a home, yet by
Its very discipline we can ensure
That nothing wasteful is allowed to lie
Within. Each phrase is weighed and polished 'til
It shines, and, as the thought is likened to
A point, so must each chosen word distil
Its essence wholly to this single view.
A small and shining house that offers rest;
A sanctuary wherein the mind finds space;
A place of light that greets each welcome guest
With care and nourishment that spring from grace.
A thought has boundaries whilst running free,
Yet, under law, knows perfect liberty.

XXXIV

A willingness to yield my treasured will;
Acceptance of a curb on my desires;
A recognition that I will fulfil
Your plan for me; can this be love? The fires
Of self-willed passion flicker and subside,
A word I hardly knew comes into play
As, from the dying embers of false pride,
A rising phoenix offers to obey.
Our will I vest in you, your wishes mine;
Our trust I place in you, do what you may;
Our path I leave to you, but I will shine
My light to guide your footsteps on the way.
Can this be love, when separation dies
And unity is all I recognise?

XXXV

Come, as I sit beside your feet and rest
My head against your knees, let us recall
The day; and in the space made manifest
By joy recount to one another all
Its pleasures and anxieties. We'll share
Our lives as we were meant to do, and in
The light of love events which seem unfair
Or hurtful lose their power 'til they are thin
Pale shadows of a dream. Like flotsam cast
Upon the sea of life they cannot go
Beneath the surface sheen, nor stir the vast
Untroubled depths our hearts explore below.
Come, smile upon the day's complexity;
Our love is real, the rest mere fantasy.

XXXVI

Leaves, golden, gaily dancing on the breeze;
Leaves, crimson, pouring blood upon the grass;
Leaves, piling, furrowed deep beneath the trees,
Entice our feet to crush them as we pass.
I gathered Autumn leaves for you to share,
The finest I could find from every tree,
But when I saw their glory fading there
I knew they'd only live in memory.
Accept them, love, but see not their decay,
Each one took part in Autumn's cavalcade;
Each had its hour when, golden-skinned and gay,
It lit a flame of joy that will not fade.
Leaves, dying, end their life upon the earth;
Leaves, mouldering, give promise of rebirth.

XXXVII

The sleeping giant was wakened by a touch
And from the silence rose the organ's song;
Far off at first, a distant call of such
Clear, haunting beauty as could not belong
To instrument alone but seemed to spill
From overflowing music in our hearts.
Quickly responsive to the player's skill
It grew in volume; then, as flower starts
Unfolding to the sun, let forth such blaze
Of colour on the ear that we were caught
In breathless, motionless delight. Power stay;
Concealed within the instrument, unsought
It sleeps; yet, like our hearts, will only take
A gentle touch to bid its joy awake.

XXXVIII

Within the theatre foyer, on the wall,
There hung a gilt-edged mirror. It had been
An actor's gift, and underneath, in small
Neat lettering, the words were clearly seen:
'This glass is only able to reflect
The true and beautiful'. Attention caught,
We smiled; though in our eyes I could detect
A flicker of relief as each one sought,
And found, his mirrored face. Yet once we knew,
When seeing life through cloudless, infant eyes,
That all of us are beautiful and true.
Now, in a looking-glass, we recognise
Forgotten truths returning from afar
And, briefly, see ourselves for what we are.

XXXIX

She sits there, fingering her wedding-ring
With restless hands, while counsel for the Crown,
Urbane and skilled, concludes his questioning.
She listens, keen and anxious, quick to frown
At each obtrusive sound that might distract
The judge's ear. They speak of violence
In passive tones, as men play out an act
They've played before; where one man's innocence
Or guilt is held contained within the scope
And framework of the law. Did this man kill?
I watch as one apart, untouched by hope
Or senseless craving for revenge, until
I see the words: 'Imprisonment for life'
Inflict their sentence on the prisoner's wife.

XL

The country offers shelter to the stars;
Or so it seems to city eyes who know
Of neon's pallid rivalry and cars'
Fierce headlamps burning up the night. Below
The awesome dome of pastoral skies the black
Lies deep. Each step is an adventure for
We know not where we tread, and rough the track
Where every stone looms larger than before.
Here nature's laws dictate when day is spent;
Here darkness shows more clearly than the light
The sweeping vistas of the firmament
That lends its sequined splendour to the night.
Let me remember in the city glare
That somewhere, hung in space, the stars are there.

XLI

What if there never was a virgin birth,
No cattle bearing witness to the sight;
What if no angels sang of peace on earth,
No star shone tribute in the winter's night?
What if it were a dream? Would aught remain
Within the ashes of a cherished myth
To raise the cry "Hosannah!" and sustain
Man's soaring spirit on the wings of faith?
I know not, Lord, what history would flout
But Christmas bids us leave our flocks for thee,
And calls us through the darkness of our doubt
Towards the light of thy nativity.
We need not journey to a distant inn
When faith, and hope, and love are born within.

XLII

All men can love, but few are resolute
To stand by what they know in times of strain.
All men have strength, but many would refute
Their manly fortitude when faced with pain.
All men have eyes to see and lips to praise,
But yours, my darling, know no boundary;
Distilling from the essence of your days
The living spirit of your poetry.
All men have arms, but I have never known
Two arms as tender and as dear as yours.
All men can smile, but on your face is shown
The inner beauty that your nature stores.
Of all the men I've met why should it be
That you, my darling, fell in love with me?

XLIII

I love the way your lips twitch when I speak
To show a smile is twinkling within;
I love the glow that deepens in your cheek
When impish teasing prompts a boyish grin.
I love the gentle touch of powerful hands,
The natural grace of manhood in its prime,
The joy of knowing someone understands—
And has been understanding all the time.
Your tender smile my restless spirit soothes,
Your circling arms are home and dwelling place;
In love-lapped happiness my finger smooths
The finely-chiselled beauty of your face.
You are the rock I turn to in distress
For nothing is as strong as gentleness.

XLIV

Sleep cradled in my arms, that I may see
Your much-loved face in slumber on my breast;
Lay worldly cares aside, entrust to me
The function of protector whilst you rest.
As acorn shelters in the Winter earth,
As from the womb the babe draws nourishment,
As spirit rests in Self before rebirth,
Let my embrace restore your heart's content.
Refreshed once more you'll waken to obey
The call of truth down paths I can't foresee;
Man hears the call of home at close of day,
Return when darkness falls, take rest in me.
Sleep in my arms 'til earthly worries cease,
You are my knowledge, let me be your peace.

XLV

How is it that a heart so full of love
Can yet find room enough to love you more;
And boundless admiration still improve
By daily growing deeper than before?
You never told me, dear, that every hour
Would bring to light fresh facets of the truth;
That time, in passing, would bestow the power
And strength of manhood on the charm of youth.
Though many moons have waned since first we met
Each fresh encounter wakens love anew;
How could I momentarily forget
The miracle of being loved by you?
No matter that my heart should overflow
For I would tell the world I love you so.

XLVI

Postscript

Pure music stems from perfect instrument;
Clear liquid from a spotless jug must flow;
So how can I, with groping words, present
In their simplicity the truths I know?
How may a stumbling tongue express the sound
That nature's chorus holds in unity?
Can restless minds find stillness to expound
The inner nourishment of peace? Give me
But time; let me this instrument refine;
Help me to cleanse the vessel of the mind
That from it I may pour you truth's pure wine
Leaving all sediment dissolved behind.
Until that day, accept these gifts I bring,
For even husky voices need to sing.

Notes and Acknowledgements

Sonnet

XVI: Winner of first place in the Literary Composition Class at the Worthing Music Festival 1973.

XXIII: In memory of Emily Hull of Chiddingfold.

XXIV: In tribute to the Floral Festival at Tickenham Parish Church, Somerset.

XXV: First published in *Keats Prize Poems* and reproduced by courtesy of London Literary Editions.

XXIX: First published in *Horizon* the magazine of the Cinque Port Poets.

XXXII: In tribute to the work of Mrs. Pansy Irish of Nevada, and reproduced here with her kind permission.

XLVI: The property of The Music Therapy Charity Limited, and reproduced here with their kind permission.

I would like to add my gratitude to Mrs. May Griffith Edwards for kindly and painstakingly studying this collection and contributing much invaluable advice.